FEEDING
BACKYARD BIRDS

Scott Edwards

Photo Credits:

Ron Austing: p. 3 (Painted Bunting); 6B; 35 (chipmunk); 38T; 40; 44T & B; 45TC; 47C; 50; 55 (European Starling); 57; 58
Jeff Fishbein: p. 6T; 7; 12; 14B; 17; 42; 46T & B
Marvin Hyett: p. 23 (Carolina Chickadee); 52T
Kaytee Products: p. 44BC; 45BC; 47T
Larry Kimball: p. 14T; 22; 25; 45B; 47B
Larry Kimball & Barbara Magnuson: p. 18; 51 (House Wren)
Barbara Magnuson: p. 5 (Western Bluebird); 30B; 37T
Rafi Reyes: p. 8; 11 all; 19 all; 20; 24; 26T; 27 all; 28B; 29T & B; 30T; 52B; 53T; 54; 59
Rob & Ann Simpson: p. 1 (Carolina Chickadee); 9 (American Robin); 10; 21; 31; 34; 37B; 38B; 44TC; 45T; 46C; 49; 53B (columbine); 62
John Tyson: p. 4; 41; 43 (Tufted Titmouse); 56
Maleta M. Walls: p. 26B; 28T; 29C; 32 all; 33; 53

Dedication

To Pete Dunne, who for many years never let one of our conversations go without asking about my book, or telling me there was a book there, go write it. For always thinking more of me than I did myself. And for making me a part of the greatest Audubon Society on the planet, New Jersey Audubon.

To my daughter, Sierra, for each and every day making me want to be a better person and for reminding me my work is not just for now, but for future generations as well.

To My Mom......'nuff said

KT 100

Distributed in the UNITED STATES to the Pet Trade by T.F.H. Publications, Inc., 1 TFH Plaza, Neptune City, NJ 07753; on the Internet at www.tfh.com; in CANADA by Rolf C. Hagen Inc., 3225 Sartelon St., Montreal, Quebec H4R 1E8; Pet Trade by H & L Pet Supplies Inc., 27 Kingston Crescent, Kitchener, Ontario N2B 2T6; in ENGLAND by T.F.H. Publications, PO Box 74, Havant PO9 5TT; in AUSTRALIA AND THE SOUTH PACIFIC by T.F.H. (Australia), Pty. Ltd., Box 149, Brookvale 2100 N.S.W., Australia; in NEW ZEALAND by Brooklands Aquarium Ltd., 5 McGiven Drive, New Plymouth, RD1 New Zealand; in SOUTH AFRICA by Rolf C. Hagen S.A. (PTY.) LTD., P.O. Box 201199, Durban North 4016, South Africa; in JAPAN by T.F.H. Publications. Published by T.F.H. Publications, Inc.

Manufactured in the

United States of America

by T.F.H. Publications, Inc.

CONTENTS

A male American Goldfinch in breeding color.

Introduction

WHY FEED
THE BIRDS?

People feed birds for a number of different reasons. One thing is clear, however: many people are doing it. In fact, recent government studies show that one out of every four people in the United States feeds the birds.

One reason for feeding is very simple. Birds are beautiful to look at. Virtually nowhere else in nature can one see such color and variety: Northern Cardinals with their bright red plumage, American Goldfinches the color of pure sunshine, and, as Thoreau so aptly put it, the bluebird that carries the sky on his back.

Other people feed birds because they are looking for a lost connection to the natural world. There is a sense

Birds such as this Northern Cardinal should be fed to be enjoyed, not through any sense of obligation.

of tranquillity and order to knowing that no matter what is happening in our busy world, the birds are still going about their lives as they have for centuries. A feeder filled with birds reinforces the sense that nature persists. What a wonderful way to start the day—get up in the morning, look outside, and watch the birds come to a feeder for "breakfast." It really doesn't matter where you are—city, suburb, countryside—birds are everywhere. Birds are typically more than appreciative guests, dining wherever and whenever a repast is laid out before them.

One reason that people *shouldn't* feed the birds is out of a false sense of obligation that the birds would starve without a constant supply of birdseed. This simply isn't the case. On average, birds get about 20 percent of their daily caloric intake from birdseed. Birds have a very high metabolism and need to eat a well-balanced diet, so they seek and gain nourishment from many sources: fruits, nuts, insects, and flowers among them. They also eat a variety of different seeds in nature, some providing nutrients not found in commercial birdseed.

Many people do not realize that seed-eating birds make up only a small fraction of the birdlife that surrounds us. In fact, a number of birds cannot be coaxed to feeders at all. Another way we know that birds can survive without us is by watching them during mild winters. If it is not cold and birds are not burning calories trying to keep warm, birdseed consumption tends to drop off. This is because during the winter their job is simply to keep warm and make it to next spring to breed again. The birds just don't have a lot to do (no nesting, feeding young, etc.).

Some birds, such as Cedar Waxwings, seldom or never respond to seeds in feeders.

Another misconception about feeding birds is that feeding should be discontinued once the weather turns warmer—that the birds "need to learn to fend for themselves," that they will become "dependent" on our feeders if we feed all year long. In fact, birds actually eat more birdseed during the spring and summer months than during an average winter. The reason for this is twofold: 1) natural seed supplies have not yet replenished themselves from the previous autumn when the plants went to seed; 2) birds become more intrinsically tied to our yards due primarily to breeding responsibilities. In the spring, birds fight to establish territories, attract a mate, build a nest, brood, and raise young. If they have to venture too far afield for food, all that they have worked for can be quickly lost. In actuality, our feeders become the avian equivalent of a fast-food restaurant. Parent birds work hard all day at the job of parenting and will stop off for a quick bite at our feeders to keep them going. There has never been any sound scientific evidence to support the suspension of birdfeeding in warm weather. In fact, if you do stop feeding as soon as the weather turns mild and don't start again until the first icy blast of winter, you are missing one of nature's greatest phenomena: migration. Every spring, millions of birds move from their wintering grounds in the south to their breeding grounds in the north; in the fall they do the reverse. For people in many areas, this is the only time to see certain species at feeders. Summer is also the time of year that American Goldfinches are dressed in their bright yellow plumage; it's also when hummingbirds are present in many parts of the country.

One of the nicest things about birdfeeding is that it is a relaxing hobby that can be done at your own comfort level of involvement. Whether you are just scattering some seed on the ground or you have a dozen or more feeders in your yard, you're feeding the birds. It's up to you to decide how involved you'd like to be. A later chapter will discuss the benefits of using feeders.

Feeding birds can also be a wonderful way to introduce children to the natural world. What could be more fascinating to a child than something brightly colored that flies and sings beautiful songs—and is right in their own backyard? It can lead to a lifetime of appreciation and love of nature. Feeding birds can also be a great way to teach children responsibility. Give them their own feeder and have them keep it full and clean. It will give them a connection to the birds and nature and a sense of accomplishment when the birds show up regularly.

A Hairy Woodpecker taking peanut butter from a feeding rack. Peanut butter is eaten by many birds and often is mixed with seeds in place of suet.

Whatever your reason for feeding the birds, remember that it should be a source of enjoyment, a chance to bring the most colorful and vibrant creatures in all of nature right to your window. You will come to know your regular visitors and look forward to their arrival each day. You'll marvel as the fledglings follow their parents to your feeder and beg for a morsel of seed. Your eyes will widen as unexpected and breathtaking guests put in an appearance on fine spring days. Soon, you will learn to love it.

Any garden, no matter how attractive, draws more birds if feeders are present.

Chapter One

GETTING STARTED

Once you've decided that birdfeeding is something you'd like to do, you'll need some direction on the best way to get started. First, take a good look at your yard. Take note of the kind of trees and shrubs around your property and even in neighboring yards. Perhaps most importantly, try to identify the birds you see in your yard before the addition of any feeders. It is always a good idea to cater to the "regular customers" rather than market a yard strictly to the "tourist trade." In other words, work on getting the birds that already call your yard home to come to the feeders you put out rather than directing your efforts toward luring migrants into your habitat.

The best place to start is with a field guide to the birds of your area. Many will tell you if the birds will use feeders or not. They will also let you know if the particular species is a bird that breeds in your area or is only a seasonal resident. So, before running out and purchasing a half dozen feeders, a biological survey of your yard is in order.

Setting Up a Feeding Station

Because it is nearly impossible to find one feeder that will attract and work for all the birds in your yard, a combination of three or four feeders will work best. The term used for this kind of setup is a

A feeding station with a typical variety of feeders.

"feeding station." The most important thing about your feeding station is to set it up where you can see it. Far too many people are overly concerned with other aspects of feeder placement, such as cover, and are then unable to view their feeders. (Author's note: using the term cover often leads people to believe that their feeder must be stuck in the bushes to be successful. One of the most active feeders in my front yard is 25 feet from the nearest brush.) You need to be ready to accept the fact that you may have to "walk your birds in" to a prime viewing area. If you have never fed before, sticking your very first feeder right on the busiest window of your house will most likely not have the results you wish. Start with a feeder within easy reach of any trees and cover, yet far enough away to exclude squirrels. As the birds get used to the feeder and recognize it as a source of food, you can slowly move it closer and closer to your chosen viewing area. Experiment with your feeder location, but don't tamper with it every day. When a feeder is not performing up to expectations, the easiest and most economical variable to consider is location. If it doesn't work, move it. But, make sure you have given your feeder ample time, two to three weeks on average, before relocating it. Always remember that this is for enjoyment. Find a favorite place to sit and work toward putting your feeders outside those windows. Kitchens and breakfast areas are always a good choice because you're able to observe the birds in the morning when they are most active, fueling up to start their day. The next step is to think about the kinds of feeders that will round out your feeding station.

HOPPER FEEDERS

A good way to start your backyard feeding is with a well-designed hopper feeder, basically a covered platform feeder that has a hopper, or receptacle, inside to hold seed and dispense it gradually. Many people like these feeders because they hold large amounts of seed and are attractive to a wide variety of birds. In fact, hopper feeders are second only to fly-through style platform feeders in terms of the number of different species they will attract.

Many people feel that a station should have at least a tube feeder for sunflower, one for nyjer, and a hopper or platform feeder.

There are several key features to look for in the construction of a hopper feeder. Adequate drainage is critical; the feeder should have a screen bottom or several holes drilled in the bottom to allow rainwater to drain and to facilitate the flow of air around the seed, allowing it to dry out once wet. A feeder screwed together (not nailed or stapled) will go a long way to providing you with years of trouble-free use. Feeders that are not built properly tend to fall apart quickly and don't represent a good value. Staples and nails tend to pull out, the wood is more likely to split, and your feeder is destined for a much earlier replacement than one made of at least half-inch thick cedar with zinc chromate or brass hardware. Yes, these features are initially more expensive, but they assure you of a soundly designed, long-lasting product. Also, a manufacturer that has invested time and effort into designing and producing an attractive feeder is much more likely to build it properly than one that just throws something together.

This hopper feeder sits on a wide platform.

Other important elements include a good-sized roof to protect the feeding area and a large open feeding area to accommodate a large variety of birds and allow the unobstructed flow of seed. You should avoid hopper feeders with small holes that the seed is

11

A Northern Cardinal and an Evening Grosbeak feed at the dish beneath a tube feeder.

supposed to come out of. These tend to dam, leaving the birds unable to get to the seed. A hopper feeder with the aforementioned components will allow both the birds and you to benefit from years of feeding enjoyment.

TUBE FEEDERS

The next style of feeder suited for a well-rounded feeding station is the tube feeder. A tube feeder usually consists of a plastic or Lexan tube with holes or "ports" in it and perches to allow the birds a place to land and feed. The nyjer feeder also falls into the tube feeder category, but uses unusually small ports to allow more controlled flow of nyjer.The advantages of using tube feeders are as follows: 1) the tube material is almost always clear, allowing the birds (and you) to see the amount of seed inside. This also adds to the overall attractiveness of the feeder. 2) By their very nature, tube feeders are "species exclusive." What this means is that their design does not allow easy access to some birds, particularly the larger ones. Blue Jays, Starlings, grackles, and cardinals find the perches on tube feeders to be a bit on the small side. Of course, this design can be both a blessing and a curse. If you are using a tube feeder as a part of a comprehensive feeding station, you may very well want to exclude the larger birds, providing an undisturbed feeding area for your finches, chickadees, titmice, and smaller woodpeckers. However, if a tube feeder is your only feeder, you may be disappointed in the absence of some of the larger and more colorful birds. But take heart, there are ways to customize your tube feeder to accommodate the larger visitors to your yard.The simplest way to allow more diversity at this type of feeder is with the addition of a seed tray, which is nothing more than a shallow plastic dish designed to fit on the bottom of your tube. It allows cardinals, doves, jays, the larger woodpeckers, and other birds that are uncomfortable on perches to land on the tray and feed from the lower ports. Be aware, however, that this feature may mean that your feeder is emptied more rapidly than you wish. Fortunately, due to the popularity of the design, manufacturers are making much larger tube feeders, as well as those with trays permanently built in. Tube feeders should be filled exclusively with black oil sunflower. Birds that frequent this style of feeder are only looking for sunflower and will quickly deposit millet and other seeds on the ground via bill sweeping, the process by which some birds flick seeds aside in order to find their favorite seed in a mix. Tube feeders are usually hung from tree branches, ideally well out of the reach of leaping squirrels, but more on dealing with these charming fellows later.

PLATFORM FEEDERS

The most attractive feeder to many birds is the platform, or fly-through, feeder. These are open trays, either with or without a roof, that the birds have full access to. The benefits of such a design are obvious—the birds find these feeders much easier to land on, they have no problems with seed dispensing, and they come and go from whichever direction they feel most comfortable. A major advantage of the platform feeder is that there is no dispensing system to be clogged, and you are free to feed virtually any type of food you want, from sunflower seed and suet to fruit and peanuts in the shell. The disadvantage of such a design is the lack of any carrying capacity; that is, the platform feeder needs more regular filling.

This style of feeder is also one that requires the most drainage due to its design, especially if you choose one with an uncovered platform. Screen or mesh bottoms are essential for a feeder of this sort to perform at its best. It is also important to clean debris off this feeder regularly so as not to clog the drainage openings.

A gourmet seed mix will help you attract a wide variety of garden birds, from cardinals and finches to woodpeckers. Photo courtesy of Kaytee® Products, Inc.

Ground feeders such as Mourning Doves and many sparrows are best served by a low platform feeder just inches above the ground.

GROUND FEEDERS

A variation on the platform/fly-through feeder is the ground feeder, which is a platform positioned low enough to the ground to attract birds that rarely leave the ground. Sparrows, juncos, towhees, and doves prefer to feed on or near the ground. These just happen also to be the birds that prefer white proso millet, which obviously makes your ground feeder a perfect place for this seed. Drainage is just as important in a ground feeder as it is in a fly-through or platform feeder. Wet, moldy birdseed is a breeding ground for germs and diseases and should be avoided at all costs. Seed that starts to smell should be discarded immediately. Ground feeders are preferable to scattering seed on the ground due to the fact that they keep the seed drier and less likely to be wasted.

SUET FEEDERS

Suet feeders are also a welcome addition to your feeding station. Suet, specifically, is the fat that surrounds beef kidney. Most of what is available today is the commercial variety, which has been rendered to prevent it from going rancid. These suet cakes are designed to fit into cages made for hanging suet on the trunks of trees. Beware of the "suet" that is available at most grocery stores in the meat department. What you are usually getting is the unrendered trimmings from other cuts of meat. This variety will allow the fat to turn bad; it is also often combined with a low-quality seed mix to add to its attractiveness to the consumer, while doing little for the birds. Stick with the suet products packaged for

Suet is known for attracting woodpeckers and nuthatches. Here an elegant Pileated Woodpecker visits a suet cake.

birdfeeding; they are readily available and their convenience and resistance to spoiling make them worth the extra few cents.

When you initially offer suet to the birds, hang it in a suet cage or bag on the trunk of a large deciduous tree. This is where birds that eat suet make their living. Birds such as woodpeckers, titmice, chickadees, creepers, and nuthatches glean insects from the bark of these trees, excavate and/or use cavities in them for nesting, and basically spend most of their life perched on the trunk of a tree. Your odds for success in attracting birds to suet will be much higher if you present it this way. The odds of having a woodpecker just happen to find a basket dangling in space are not very good, and it is also very difficult for the larger woodpeckers to comfortably accomplish the feat of landing on the basket. By mounting it on the trunk of a tree, you are allowing the birds to use the tree itself as the landing platform, instead of trying to balance themselves on a swinging basket.

Suet cakes are available in a myriad of flavors, and it can be fun to try the different kinds to see which your birds prefer. One word of caution, however: what is added to the suet in the way of seed, nuts, berries, peanut butter, etc., will also make your suet attractive to squirrels. Pure suet is commercially available and is, for the most part, significantly less attractive to squirrels.

WINDOW STRIKES

A question that often comes up regarding window feeders is that of "window strike," which is when a bird flies into a window. Believe it or not, window feeders actually help deter window strike, rather than increase it. Window strike is most often caused when startled or frightened birds look quickly for a path to get away and head for a reflection of the sky and trees in the window. Window feeders actually break up that reflection, thereby lessening the chance of impact.

WINDOW FEEDERS

Once you start attracting birds to your yard, it is only natural to want to get a closer view of your avian guests. One very easy way to accomplish this is with the addition of a window feeder to your feeding station. Window feeders are most often made of Lexan or plastic and stick to the outside of your windows via a set of good suction cups. Perhaps the two most asked questions regarding window feeders are: 1) Will the birds actually come right up to my window? and 2) Do they really stick? The answer to both these questions is a resounding yes. Birds are incredibly adaptive creatures and, given the proper amount of patience, will come to your window and even begin to ignore your presence. You can facilitate how quickly the birds warm up to your window feeder with several methods. One is to initially put the window feeder on a window that gets less passerby traffic than most. By doing so, you limit the number of times you scare the birds off the feeder. The other way to get the birds to come more quickly is the application of a "two-way" mirror panel. Many feeders come with these built in or available as an accessory. Although they don't totally block your presence, they will mask your movement to a great degree. In regard to getting your window feeder to adhere to your window, fight your impulse to lick the suction cups to get them to stick. While this may work great at first, it will not last long. As soon as the saliva evaporates, air takes its place and your feeder comes down. A thin film of oil is generally recommended for getting suction cups to stick. Either rub the suction cups on your forehead or use a tiny amount of vegetable oil. Anything more than that will oversaturate the suction cups and cause the feeder to slide down the window.

PEANUT FEEDERS

Peanut feeders are a relatively new addition to the world of feeders and are designed to offer whole peanut pieces (not the very fine peanut hearts) to nut-loving birds like chickadees, titmice, nuthatches, jays, and woodpeckers. The feeders themselves are made of metal screening or mesh; the birds peck at the peanut kernels and eat them right there. Many people believe that if the bird cannot immediately extract the nut, the feeder is not working properly. However, the birds that enjoy nuts do not have the ability to sit there and eat a peanut the way a finch or cardinal eats a sunflower seed. They are forced to fly away with the peanut and either hold it between their feet or wedge it into the bark of a tree to start eating it. With feeders designed so that peanuts cannot be pulled out immediately, we are able to watch birds eat that we normally would only

Continued on Page 20

Many choices in birdseeds, from basic mixes to specialty blends, as well as bells and cakes, are available. Choose what is right for your yard and the birds you wish to attract. Photo courtesy of Kaytee® Products, Inc.

A White-breasted Nuthatch feeding from a peanut feeder.

Squirrel-proof Feeders

Perhaps the most hotly debated topic in all of birdfeeding is that of the squirrel-proof feeder. The Gray Squirrel, which inhabits a large percentage of backyards, evokes a gamut of emotions, from rage to affection and everything in between. Some people place special feeders out that actually cater to the squirrels, while others go to great lengths to rid their yard of these all-time-greatest seed thieves.

To begin with, "squirrel-proof" means different things to different people. To some manufacturers, it means the squirrel can't hurt the feeder but can pilfer seed from it. To others it means that all efforts have been made to prevent the squirrel from eating any of the seed. It is also important to note that a lot of squirrel-proof feeders also exclude some birds. That's because whatever design feature makes them inaccessible to squirrels also makes them unattractive or inaccessible to larger birds, such as cardinals.

Heavy, open mesh around a feeder may slow feeding by squirrels and other unwanted large animals, such as this Pinyon Jay.

There are two basic designs for squirrel-proof feeders. The first is the caged feeders, which are those with wire cages around them. This design favors clinging birds such as House Finches, goldfinches, chickadees, titmice, and woodpeckers, all of which are able to simply reach through the cage and pull out some sunflower. Another style of caged feeder is one in which the smaller birds are actually able to hop inside to eat. These are generally considered more squirrel-proof than the basic cage design because the seed tube is located far enough away from the cage that the squirrel will probably not be able to gain access to the seed. This is by far the most species-exclusive design, allowing only the smaller finches, chickadees, and titmice to feed. The second kind of squirrel-proof feeder, which allows a wider variety of

If the feeder is far enough from a branch or roof, a squirrel guard around the post may discourage squirrels.

birds to feed, is the spring-loaded feeder. These feeders are usually constructed of steel to keep squirrels from chewing their way in. They also have a large landing platform supported by springs strong enough to support a bird's light weight but shut down under a squirrel's. The landing platform then lowers another piece of metal over the feeding area, effectively cutting off the squirrels from the feed supply. Although these types of feeders have proven highly effective in thwarting squirrels, it is worthwhile to note that there is no such thing as 100 percent squirrel-proof. Our best hope lies in slowing them down as much as possible.

Not only do squirrels steal and waste food, but they often are very destructive of the feeders themselves. Even if a feeder is empty, they still can smell the seed and will think there is more food.

American Goldfinches may be the main reason that many birders provide nyjer tube feeders for the birds.

see as a fleeting glimpse. One of the best features of a peanut feeder is that it is not usually overwhelmed by finches.

NYJER (THISTLE) FEEDER

A variation on the tube feeder design is the nyjer (formerly niger) feeder. Although this feeder has often been referred to as a "thistle" feeder, the seed put through these tube feeders with tiny openings is actually nyjer, which is imported into this country and is sterilized to prevent it from germinating. This combination of freight costs and extra labor is the reason why nyjer is often referred to as "black gold" in birdfeeding lingo.

The primary reason for adding a nyjer feeder to your feeding station is to attract goldfinches, Pine Siskins, and redpolls—but, most of all, American Goldfinches, whose bright yellow breeding plumage is a favorite of birdfeeders during the spring and summer months. Goldfinches like nyjer more than most other birds, even though they would rather have sunflower. Because Goldfinches prefer to eat alone, the best results from offering nyjer come when you place your feeder slightly outside the heavy flight zone of your feeding station. Although they will battle fiercely with one another for a seat on a feeder, they beat a hasty retreat when confronted by larger birds, especially House Finches. In fact, there is even a feeder available that offers nyjer upside down, with the feeding ports located below the perches. Although American Goldfinches have no problem with this feat, House Finches have a very difficult time gaining any food from this feeder, thereby leaving your "black gold" for the birds you intended it for. Nyjer feeders are also, for the most part, unattractive to squirrels and can be placed in areas you would otherwise not be able to hang a feeder.

HUMMINGBIRD FEEDERS

An even more specialized feeder for your feeding station is one designed specifically for hummingbirds. Hummingbird feeders differ greatly from the previously mentioned feeders in that they dispense "nectar," typically in the form of a sugar-water solution. These types of feeders come in two common basic styles, the inverted bottle and the saucer. Both have their advantages and disadvantages. The inverted bottle design allows you to put out less nectar during extremely warm spells, thereby wasting less of it (nectar spoils quickly in heat). The drawback to virtually every inverted bottle design is how difficult they are to clean. The saucer variety is becoming more and more popular due to its ease of care; however, it needs to be kept full so that hummingbirds can reach the nectar.

Nectar is nothing more than a sugar and water mixture—four parts water to one part sugar—boiled and then cooled. You can make extra nectar and keep it in the refrigerator for a week or so. There is no need to add food coloring to the nectar because any hummingbird feeder worth putting up will be brightly colored enough to attract the birds. It is important to stress, however, that you must keep your nectar fresh and your feeder clean. The sugar-water solution can ferment rapidly on hot days. In fact, during extensive heat waves it might be advisable not to put your feeders out at all, as the nectar could easily go bad in just a day or so.

This introduction to feeders is well rounded but by no means all-inclusive. There are thousands of feeders on the market today, some better than others. Look for longevity from a feeder, not an ultra-low price. Quality is generally not inexpensive, and a well-designed and well-built feeder will serve you for many years. Take a good look at your yard and decide which feeders will work best for you and then put them up and await your guests.

To attract hummingbirds (here Broad-billed Hummingbirds), provide a simple sugar solution in plain water (1:4) and serve in a red hummingbird feeder.

A pair of Red Crossbills at a large-capacity open-mesh feeder.

Chapter Two

SEEDS:
KEEPING IT SIMPLE

The bags are adorned with colorful birds, a promise of color and variety the likes of which most of us who feed birds only dream of. Pictured are Cedar Waxwings, a handful of warblers, and a number of other birds that have never made it to the pages of any field guide. The fact is, the number of birds that actually consume seed is a small percentage of our avian population, and no amount of exotic seeds, dried fruits, or other ingredients is going to drastically change what comes to our birdfeeders.

What you should look for in your bag of birdseed, regardless of which birds are pictured on the bag, is a very simple mixture of seeds. First and foremost in

Hulled sunflower seeds produce little waste on the ground to attract pigeons and mice.

any seed mixture should be black oil sunflower. You can check the ingredients listing either on a tag sewn to the bottom of the bag or printed on the back; ingredients are always listed in order of percentage in the mix. Black oil sunflower should always be the first ingredient listed, because it is the one seed most readily consumed by the birds that frequent feeders. Those with any other ingredient listed first may be designed for price, not attractiveness to the birds. Other acceptable ingredients are black stripe sunflower, white proso millet, sunflower chips or hearts, and nuts, such as peanuts, almonds, or filberts. In some instances, white proso millet doesn't belong in a seed mix, because the birds that prefer millet prefer it on or near the ground, and certain styles of feeders discourage these birds from using them. The birds that do use the feeders sweep the millet out, putting it on the ground anyway. This isn't necessarily a bad thing, but it means that your feeders will be emptied more quickly. Millet is best served on a ground feeder in close proximity to a brush pile, which is where the sparrows, juncos, towhees, and doves that want it prefer to feed. It is a good idea not only to know what the birds want to eat, but where they want to eat it. Sunflower and nuts go up in the air, millet on the ground. It really is that simple.

You may also want to provide peanuts in a feeder by themselves. This will give you a feeder that will be primarily for chickadees, titmice, nuthatches, and woodpeckers and one that won't be mobbed by the omnipresent House Finch. There are a variety of feeders on the market today made expressly to feed peanut kernels. The smaller peanut hearts are not an ingredient you want in your mix because these do more to attract European Starlings, considered a pest to many, than any other bird. Don't worry about chickadees and titmice needing to swallow the peanut kernels whole or get them out of the feeder too easily. These birds, as well as nuthatches, woodpeckers, and even Blue Jays, are what are often called "hit and run" feeders. They fly in, grab what they want, and fly off to eat it by placing it between their feet and hammering it open or breaking it into more manageable pieces. The peanut kernel feeders actually are designed to hold the peanut kernel so that the bird will sit there longer and eat right there, allowing you to watch them longer.

Two other seeds that are fine for feeding, but ought to be fed on their own and not in mixes, are safflower and nyjer (thistle). Safflower in and of itself is not a very attractive birdseed and adds no value to a mix. However, fed by itself, safflower can be quite the problem-solver.

Safflower is especially unattractive to European Starlings, Common Grackles, and even the omnipresent Gray Squirrel. This is especially helpful during the late spring and summer, when grackles and starlings are in the midst of their breeding season and can tend to overwhelm your feeders. Chickadees, Tufted Titmice, House Finches, and especially Northern Cardinals learn to relish safflower seed. Safflower should be offered in one feeder year-round to keep the birds accustomed to it. It is also a terrific seed for window feeders, keeping them for the birds many of us wish to see most.

Nyjer seed, commonly referred to as thistle, is the seed offered to attract American Goldfinch; Pine Siskin, redpolls, and Purple Finch relish it as well. It too should be offered by itself in a feeder designed especially for the economical dispensing of nyjer. These feeders should be placed a bit off to the side of your main feeding area, because American Goldfinches prefer to feed in private and don't often fight for a seat with the more aggressive House Finch at the feeder.

Sunflower seeds, nuts, millet, safflower, and nyjer can all be used in efficient ways to cover your birdseed bases. Filler seeds, such as milo, wheat, oats, canary seed, flax, and ambiguous "mixed grain products" tend to get wasted, swept off the feeder and onto the ground, where they go either uneaten or attract squirrels and mice. Although buying high-quality birdseed can certainly be more expensive at the counter, it is more cost-efficient over time. With a quality product, every single seed you offer will be eaten instead of swept out of the feeder and onto the ground, where your hard-earned birdseed dollar either sprouts or gets moldy.

The Pine Siskin is one of the specialty finches that may appear only at a niger tube feeder.

Birdseed Overview

This is a quick look at what you want to find in your mixes and what you don't. The purpose of mixed birdseed should always be to increase the number of bird visits and the variety of birds visiting, not decrease cost. A good rule of thumb is not to purchase a mixed seed that is less expensive than pure black oil sunflower. This will prevent you from buying a mix in which black oil sunflower is not the primary ingredient and in which "filler" seeds have been added to fill out the bag.

BLACK OIL SUNFLOWER

BLACK OIL SUNFLOWER: The single most preferred seed you can offer. It should always be the primary ingredient (listed first) in any mixed birdseed. Cardinals, grosbeaks, chickadees, titmice, nuthatches, and finches all flock to this seed. Black oil sunflower is the cornerstone of a sound feeding program.

BLACK STRIPE SUNFLOWER: Although eaten by some of the larger birds, such as Northern Cardinals and birds in the grosbeak family, it is still not as readily eaten as black oil sunflower. It is also more difficult for birds like chickadees, titmice, and nuthatches to open. In addition, it has a lower meat-to-shell ratio than

BLACK STRIPE SUNFLOWER

oilers, meaning that there is more shell and less meat for the birds; it is also more expensive. This seed is fine in a mix, but not as the primary ingredient.

PEANUT KERNELS OR SPLITS (HALVES): These are perhaps the second most attractive food you can put out for the birds. Peanut kernels, or splits, should not be confused with the tiny "peanut hearts," the little nib that is rejected in the manufacture of peanut butter. The birds that you want to attract with peanuts— jays, woodpeckers, nuthatches,

PEANUT SPLITS

chickadees, titmice, and Northern Cardinals—prefer the kernels.

WHITE PROSO MILLET: These small pearly white seeds are most preferred by ground-feeding birds, which is why you don't put millet in tube feeders. The birds that can use a tube feeder will just sweep the millet out, forcing you to fill your feeder more often. Most sparrows, doves, juncos, towhees, buntings, and Red-winged Blackbirds are attracted to millet. It is best served either on a platform/fly-through feeder, a slightly elevated ground feeder, or broadcast directly on the ground.

MILLET

WHOLE PEANUTS: If you want to attract jays, offer whole peanuts. Jays have been known to learn the sound of whole peanuts hitting the bottom of a feeder and will come flying in from every direction. Due to their large size, whole peanuts must be offered in

WHOLE PEANUTS

open feeders; they will not pass through the dispensing system of most hopper feeders. In addition to jays, whole peanuts will also attract crows, magpies, titmice, and woodpeckers.

SAFFLOWER SEEDS

SAFFLOWER: The problem-solver seed. What makes safflower a good addition to a feeding station is not what it attracts, but what it doesn't. Safflower is not attractive to grackles, European Starlings, and squirrels. However, it loses any of that value when offered in a mix; the visitors you are trying to discourage by using safflower will still come to the mix and either sweep away the safflower to get to the other seeds or just leave it there. This is an excellent seed to offer by itself.

NYJER (THISTLE): Nyjer is another seed for offering on its own, in a specialized feeder designed for economical dispensing of this expensive seed. It is most attractive to American Goldfinches, Common Redpolls, and Pine Siskins.

NYJER

WHOLE CORN

CORN: Although jays and some woodpeckers will often consume corn, either cracked or whole, there are so many other things to offer these birds that they prefer even more. Corn, especially the cracked variety, is used primarily as a filler product. In warm, wet weather, cracked corn has a tendency to mold rapidly and is not recommended. Squirrels, on the other hand, relish a good corn snack; use corn to feed your squirrels, not your birds.

MIXED GRAIN PRODUCTS: The catchall phrase used when a birdseed mix is designed with price in mind, not for attracting birds. It can contain wheat, oats, rice, flax, milo, canary seed, and others. Although it makes a very inexpensive seed, it also makes a very unattractive seed mix. These ingredients are best avoided, as they contribute little to the success of your feeding station.

TYPICAL BIRDSEED MIX

Other Foods and Treats

It is human nature to want to try and do more for our feathered friends, but seed should really be kept to the simple rules given previously. However, there are some other things that can be added to a feeding station to help attract a wider variety of birds.

ORANGES

Many of the birds that do not eat seed can be attracted to fruit. Perhaps the most desired of these birds are the orioles, whose bright orange

An elaborate feeder for oranges and other fruits.

plumage gives away one of their feeding preferences. Many people have had success offering oranges to bring orioles into their line of vision. Because orioles spend a great deal of their time high up in the trees, they are typically out of our normal field of view. By offering oranges, you may be able to coax them down where you are more able to enjoy them.

The way you offer oranges can be as simple or involved as you like. You can simply skewer orange halves onto horizontal branches or fence posts and let the orioles find them there. There are also commercially available fruit feeders that are usually orange in color to aid in attracting the orioles; again, the fruit is skewered onto the feeder. Some feeders go as far as to feature small indentations or cups for the addition of grape jelly, another perennial oriole favorite. One of the nicest features of oriole feeders is the number of other birds that will use them, as well as the other fruits you can employ (apples and bananas are attractive to a lot of different species). Gray Catbirds, Northern Mockingbirds, American Robins, thrashers, and tanagers have all been attracted to fruit feeders. Cardinals and Red-Bellied Woodpeckers have even been known to savor an orange from time to time. There are also a number of nectar feeders designed to attract orioles. These nectar feeders are usually bright enough in color to attract more than their fair share of hummingbirds.

Though abundant in backyards, American Robins seldom come to seeds.

Woodpeckers such as this Hairy generally seldom look at seeds and go straight for the suet, but some will try the sweet juices of apples, pears, oranges, and other fruits.

Raisins, usually served after soaking in water, will draw Northern Mockingbirds on occasion.

RAISINS

Some backyard birdfeeders have success with raisins, which are especially addicting to Northern Mockingbirds and Gray Catbirds, among others. Birdfeeding lore is replete with stories of Northern Mockingbirds all but knocking on the window for their daily ration of raisins. The attractiveness of this dried fruit is increased if you soak them in warm water overnight, then drain them well before putting them out.

NUTS

Although peanuts have long been known as a birdfeeding favorite, what isn't as widely recognized is the attractiveness of other nutmeats. Almonds, hazelnuts, walnuts, and pecans (shelled, of course) are relished by the same birds that are attracted to peanuts, if not more so. Titmice are absolutely thrilled with almonds. Woodpeckers are drawn to nutmeats offered in a fly-through or platform feeder. It is important to remember that some of the larger foods, such as some nuts, will not pass through the seed dispenser of many styles of feeder.

SUET

Many people also offer suet to their backyard birds—and not just in the winter, either. Suet is a fine year-round attractant for woodpeckers, nuthatches, chickadees, titmice, Gray Catbirds, and even the occasional Pine Warbler. Commercially available suet has been rendered in a process that removes a great deal of the impurities that allow unrendered suet to turn rancid in the summer. These cakes will get soft and greasy in the warm weather, however. For those of you who prefer not to deal with the mess sometimes associated with suet, there are two alternatives. First and foremost is to freeze your suet before putting it out. It will pop out of its packaging much more readily and be less of a chore to put out. The other option is to use "suet doughs," suet cakes especially made for feeding in

Suet given to birds must be rendered, so serve only a good brand and present it in a proper container. Use suet dough in the summer.

the warmer weather. They have more dry ingredients in them and less suet, thereby making them less prone to melting. It is worthy to note, however, that these cakes are not as dense as the suet-based cakes and do not last as long when being fed upon. They are also unsuitable for cold weather feeding (below freezing), because as they freeze they become hard and very difficult for the birds to feed from.

Some people prefer to make their own suet cakes or put out raw suet from the butcher. This is fine, but make sure you're using real kidney suet, not just plain fat. The use of raw suet in all but wintertime feeding is inadvisable because it will go rancid very quickly, even in mild weather.

BREAD

For many years a common practice has been to throw bread crumbs, as well as other table scraps, out for the birds. Unfortunately, this is really not a part of a good feeding program, because most bread crumbs, donuts, crackers, and other products are usually nothing but empty calories. Birds have a very high metabolism and a high body temperature. They therefore need to eat foods that replenish their energy in an efficient manner. Human food may also contain certain chemicals and preservatives; it only makes sense that the birds might not benefit from their inclusion.

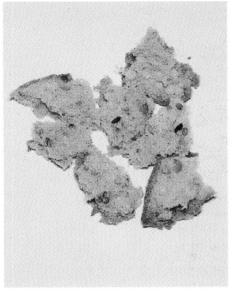

Bread, crackers, and the like are not suitable for most birds because of their high-salt, low-calorie content. Bread also attracts starlings.

NECTAR

On the topic of chemicals, nectar products for hummingbirds and orioles are another hotly debated topic. The bottom line, however, is that the addition of preservatives and dyes to these products is unnecessary. The feeders designed to dispense them are more than adequately colored to attract the desired species. The accepted mixture for these feeders is four parts plain water to one part table sugar, boiled and cooled before being put out. You can make extra and store it for a week or so in the refrigerator, so you don't have to make a fresh batch each time the feeder needs filling. This begs the question "do dyes and preservatives hurt the birds?" The answer is, we don't know. When it comes to safety at your feeding station it is always best to err on the side of caution. The birds will come to and thrive on sugar-water solutions, so stick with that.

33

A fledgling American Robin. Birds such as this often are assumed to be "abandoned."

Chapter Three

NUISANCES AT THE FEEDER

W hen you place feeders in your yard you attract not only desirable animals, but also a cross-section of all the local wildlife. Anything from chipmunks and raccoons to deer may appear to take advantage of food available at little effort.

SQUIRRELS

Expect that if you feed birds in most parts of North America, you will eventually wind up feeding squirrels as well. It's likely to happen if the proper habitat is present. Try not to let them ruin your feeding experience. In fact, when viewed with a benevolent eye, squirrels can be downright entertaining. Some people even add feeders to their yard just for the squirrels, offering nuts, sunflower, and corn on the cob for the little critters.

However, squirrels can be a formidable foe if you wish to keep them out of your birdfeeders. Fortunately, there is quite an array of products on the market to help "baffle" the squirrels. In fact, the device used to deflect squirrels from your feeder is called a baffle.

A good squirrel baffle removes the very last means of access to the feeder. It's critical to have first removed every other path, launching platform (or branch), and any other means of access by locating your feeder out of the squirrels' amazing leaping ability.

The average feeder-raiding squirrel has a vertical leap approaching and often exceeding 4 feet. They also possess a horizontal leap of 8 to 10 feet. This means you need to position your feeder at least 5 to 5 $1/2$ feet off the ground and approximately 8 to 10 feet from any overhanging limb or other spot they can jump from.

Once you have picked the ideal spot for your feeder, whether it be suspended from a branch or placed on a pole, you must now block the final means of access. This is accomplished by placing a squirrel baffle either on the pole beneath the feeder or hanging it between the feeder and the limb you have chosen. The first thing to look for in an effective squirrel baffle is size. The baffle itself must be larger than the average squirrel. A small 12-inch hanging dome-type baffle barely even slows the squirrels. In what is termed a "top attack" baffle, look for one about 18 inches in diameter and usually made of steel. Many of the less expensive squirrel baffles are made of plastic and may be chewed to pieces within the first week. If you are esthetically opposed to a large steel disc hanging in your yard and prefer a clear baffle, buy one of a high-quality material, preferably Lexan. It should be designed to be so steep that the squirrels can't sit on it and chew. The design should all but dump the squirrels onto the ground. Also, be certain that the feeder you are hanging under the baffle is not larger than the baffle itself. As the squirrel falls or jumps from the baffle, a large feeder makes an excellent claw hold. Tube feeders are usually the best choice for hanging feeders. Their very design lends them to efficient placement and offers the squirrels the least opportunity to grab onto something mid-flight.

When trying to keep squirrels from your pole-mounted feeders, the same basic rules apply. The top of your squirrel baffle needs to be approximately 4 $1/2$ feet off the ground, with a clear circle of about 8 feet around the feeder. If you cannot place your feeder safely out of the squirrel's reach, one of the squirrel-proof feeders discussed earlier is the best solution. Again, the baffle should be made of steel to avoid the squirrels gnawing their way past it. The most effective baffle design resembles a piece of stovepipe made of galvanized steel. The concept is simple: the squirrel can wrap his paws around the thinnest of poles and wires, but this type of baffle is too large in diameter for the squirrel to palm. Being made of galvanized steel, he cannot chew his way past it and, with proper placement, will not be able to hurdle it. Many a backyard feeder has enjoyed a good belly laugh watching a squirrel's tail flick around in frustration over one of these.

Another method that can be employed when dealing with squirrels is "diversionary feeding." In this method you offer squirrels a feeder of their own in the hopes that this will encourage them to leave your birdfeeders alone. Diversionary feeding helps decrease the amount of effort squirrels put into getting to your feeders but works best in conjunction with a sound baffling program. There are a

Open platform feeders may attract more squirrels than birds, especially if corn is given along with sunflower seeds.

variety of squirrel feeders on the market today, from the simple ear of corn stuck on a nail to boxes that the squirrels have to learn to open to extract their prize. Although these can help your squirrel situation, they will not solve it.

PIGEONS

Pigeons can be another nuisance at feeders in some urban/suburban areas. One pigeon really isn't that much of a problem, but they always seem to bring their entire extended family. Pigeons, being exceptionally large birds, can easily overwhelm your feeding station. They also bring appetites to match and even exceed their size.

Pigeons can be discouraged in many ways. First and foremost among these is being very careful what you put in your feeders. Birdseed with too much millet or a large percentage of filler products is going to wind up scattered all over the ground. This will greatly increase the likelihood that you start attracting pigeons. Keep the ground under your feeders as free from debris as possible when attempting to keep pigeons at bay. Seed with little or no shell is advisable in these circumstances. Sunflower chips or a "no mess" mix can help keep the amount of seed available to pigeons at a minimum.

The feral pigeon may be one of the most hated feeder nuisances. It wastes a lot of food and forces more desirable birds from the feeders.

Mourning Doves often feed on seeds thrown from a hanging feeder by other birds and squirrels.

Squirrel-proof feeders can also be pigeon-proof. The caged variety of feeders makes it extremely difficult (but not impossible) for pigeons to get at your birdseed. The spring-loaded variety will also shut off under the pigeon's considerable weight. Perhaps the best feeders to discourage pigeons are the ones that are round in shape, offering the pigeons no place to land and a moving target when they do try. Pigeons are not aerodynamically capable of landing lightly on these feeders and find them all but impossible to feed from. If you have pigeons in your area, you may be best served by using small, species-exclusive feeders. As of this writing, there is no known birdseed that is unattractive to pigeons, basically because they swallow most everything whole. Round feeders, small tube feeders, and caged feeders, plus a clean feeding area, can keep pigeons from being a real nuisance.

CATS

Yet another dilemma faced by those wishing to feed the birds is marauding cats. Cats pose one of the greatest threats to our native songbird population, and the situation is worsening. If you have cats, by all means keep them indoors. If they are already outdoor cats, they can be retrained and can be just as happy, and safer, than before. If it is your neighbor's cat that is stalking your feeders and birds, ask them as nicely as possible to please keep their cat out of your backyard.

Feral cats, cats that have been abandoned so long that they have returned to a semi-wild state, are the most common problem. Contact the local animal control commission in your area for details concerning how to deal with this burgeoning problem.

Beware of cats—they may kill more birds than any natural enemies.

In an area where you are dealing with cats, the best advice is to keep your feeders up in the air as high as feasible and away from cover where cats can lie in wait for unsuspecting birds. Use a large uncovered platform at least 5 $^1/_2$ feet in the air to keep your ground-feeding birds as safe as possible, and again, like with pigeons, try to keep the ground under your feeder debris-free.

ADDITIONAL PESTS

Other "objectionable" critters such as mice and rats can and do show up at feeding stations. Fortunately, it is usually just the local contingent of field mice that are going to be present near homes, whether you feed the birds or not. Wildlife of all kinds—birds, mice, squirrels, chipmunks, groundhogs, opossums, skunks, and anything else you care to name—are drawn to habitat. The better your habitat is, the larger the variety of wildlife you are likely to draw. Most of the time the wildlife is not of any concern. People who have had rats show up at their feeding station usually are either: 1) feeding a very inexpensive and filler-laden birdseed mix that just lies on the ground waiting for some scavenger to come pick it up; or 2) there is a compost heap nearby to which organic food products are being added. The odor of rotting food is all but irresistible to rodents, especially rats, which can sniff these things out a mile away. If you are going to compost foodstuffs, no matter where you live, it is advisable to do so in a closed container. If rats do show up at your feeding station, suspend feeding temporarily and call in a professional exterminator.

> ### FALSE: IF YOU TOUCH A BABY BIRD ITS PARENTS WILL ABANDON IT
>
> Sooner or later you are likely to come across a baby bird that has fallen from its nest. The rule of thumb is that if it has no feathers, try to put it back in its nest or take it to a licensed rehabilitator. A parent bird will not abandon a nestling because you have touched it. Birds have virtually no sense of smell and will therefore not reject a nestling due to human contact. If a nestling is feathered, it may have just fledged and should not be bothered. Even though you may not see the parent, it does know where it left its offspring—unless it is taken away by you. All things considered, it's best to adhere to a policy of non-intervention with nature.

Another situation that may arise at your feeding station, but should never be viewed as a problem, is the arrival of a hawk. Most people who feed birds have at one point or another witnessed a hawk attack in their yard. This is nothing more than your birdfeeder becoming a hawkfeeder. Sharp-shinned Hawks and Cooper's Hawks are fairly common throughout the country and their job is to prey upon songbirds. They are built differently from their cousins the soaring hawks, such as the Red-tailed Hawk.

This type of incident is truly a natural occurrence and should never in any way be interfered with. Birds of prey are an integral part of the environment; it should be much more disconcerting to never see a hawk in your yard than to occasionally lose a feeder visitor. It is also worth noting that these birds are stunningly beautiful and fabulous fliers. When you invite nature into your yard, you invite all of it, hawks included.

Sometimes other birds can be considered nuisances at your feeders, especially during the spring and summer months when breeding is taking place. The two most common "pest" birds are Common Grackles and European Starlings. When these birds descend upon your yard, your feeders will be quickly emptied, leaving nothing for the rest of your visitors. As when dealing with pigeons, species-exclusive feeders can help deter these birds. Also, the feeding of safflower seed (as always, by itself) and the use of pure suet can also assist you in making sure that there is always food for all your backyard visitors. It is important to have at least one feeder in your yard with safflower seed in it. This way, when the grackles and starlings show up each year, you won't have to go through a period of adjustment while your birds warm up to eating safflower all over again. Remember that squirrels are not terribly fond of safflower either, so a feeder just for it in a spot you normally couldn't keep squirrels out of is a great idea.

Finding an "Abandoned" Baby Bird

One last situation that is bound to come up in almost every backyard almost each and every spring and early summer is the discovery of a nestling that has fallen from its nest or a fledgling learning how to fly. People are typically anxious to help, but human efforts are not always in the bird's best interest. When you call a local bird store or nature center for help, please realize that it is their intent to help the baby bird, not congratulate you on your heroics. When someone is told that the bird must be taken to a federally licensed rehabilitator or just left alone, people often react defensively. Remember, you called someone to give you advice. Thank these folks for being honest and for giving you the correct information.

Don't be tempted to "rescue" fallen nestlings or fledglings. Keeping wild birds such as Orchard Orioles is against federal law.

A newly feathered bird is much like a three-year-old child. It leaves its nest, curious about the world around it, but is still dependent on its parents for survival. Parents teach the young bird to find food, recognize enemies, and adapt to surroundings.

With three to five fledglings to keep their eyes on, a parent bird might temporarily lose track of one. This is when people happen upon them and make the mistake of picking them up and moving them. Don't do it. Although you may not see the parent birds around, they do know where they left their offspring. If they come back and the bird is gone, they instinctively give it up for dead and move on to tending to the remaining fledglings.

If you find a newly feathered bird in your yard, watch it from a distance to see if the parent birds are in the vicinity and return to feed the fledgling. Do everything you can to leave a fledgling with its parents.

> ## WHAT TO DO IF YOU FIND A BABY BIRD
>
> - Do not cuddle the bird.
> - Place it on paper towels in a box if it's an older baby, place it on tissue in a small bowl if it is a nestling.
> - Keep the bird warm but out of direct sunlight.
> - Keep the bird away from people and pets.
> - Do not feed milk or bread to baby birds (they cannot digest it) and never squirt liquids into a bird's mouth. Birds have a small hole at the base of their tongue that leads directly to their windpipe and lungs. Squirting liquids into a bird's mouth can literally drown the bird.

If you find a naked nestling on the ground, look up. Chances are the nest it fell from is right overhead. Try and put it back in the nest. It is a myth that birds will reject offspring handled by humans. At best, birds have a rudimentary sense of smell, and they will not abandon a bird because of human odor. If placing the naked nestling back in the nest is out of the question and you feel you must intercede, the proper action is to take the bird to a licensed rehabilitation center. Baby birds need intensive and professional care. Rehabilitators go through exhaustive training to learn how to care for birds and release them back into the wild.

American Robin nestlings often fall from their nest and are fed by the parents while on the ground.

All in all, the best advice is to adhere to a policy of non-interference. Birds are much better prepared and equipped to care for their young than are people. Unfortunately, the good intentions of people often lead to the unnecessary death of young birds. Let nature take its course and intervene only in dire circumstances.

Don't be afraid to try new foods. This Red-bellied Woodpecker is enjoying almonds.

Chapter Four

FEEDER BIRDS AND THEIR PREFERENCES

With over 700 species of birds found regularly in the United States and Canada, it should come as no surprise that dozens of species may turn up at backyard feeders. Many birds are restricted in their distribution or breed far to the north of most populated areas, appearing in the U.S. only during migrations and winter. A large number of birds, however, have surprisingly wide ranges in North America and can be seen in backyards from California to New York. Still other types of birds look so much alike that the casual feeder is unlikly to notice that there are several species involved.

The following selection is designed to familiarize you with the most common, most observable birds and bird groups.

HOUSE FINCH

HOUSE FINCH: Will visit most any style of feeder, although they have a fondness for tube-style feeders filled with black oil sunflower. Will also consume nyjer seed, sunflower chips, and safflower.

PURPLE FINCH

PURPLE FINCH: About the same preferences as their more boisterous cousin, the House Finch. Drawn to tube feeders filled with oilers and nyjer. Will also visit safflower.

AMERICAN GOLDFINCH

AMERICAN GOLDFINCH: A smaller cousin to the House Finch, shares similar tastes in seeds. Prefers tube-style feeders to all others. Goldfinches are the main reason people feed nyjer seed. Although the American Goldfinch would rather have sunflower, they seem to enjoy nyjer better than the rest of the common backyard birds.

CAROLINA CHICKADEE

CHICKADEES: Prefer small feeders that they can cling to. Demonstrate a strong preference to black oil sunflower, peanuts, and suet. Will also develop a taste for safflower seeds.

TITMICE: Show a strong propensity for nut feeders. Especially relish peanuts, almonds, and hazelnuts. Like their kinfolk, the chickadees, titmice love feeders they can cling to.

TUFTED TITMOUSE

REDPOLLS: Mostly attracted to tube feeders designed to dispense nyjer seed. Also fond of sunflower chips and black oil sunflower seed.

COMMON REDPOLL

NORTHERN CARDINAL: Perennial favorite of birdfeeders in the East, they love black oil sunflower seeds, peanuts, and black striped sunflower; will develop a taste for safflower. Prefers feeders with large open landing areas; not a frequent visitor to tube feeders without feeding trays attached.

NORTHERN CARDINAL, IMMATURE

GROSBEAKS: No other bird can go through a feeder as fast as a member of this family of seedeaters, which live up to their name. "Grosbeaks" (great beaks) shuck sunflower seed faster than most people can put it out. Being relatively large birds, they prefer large hopper and fly-through feeders. They can also be attracted to large tube feeders with seed trays attached.

EVENING GROSBEAK

MOURNING DOVE

DOVES: Mourning Doves, Rock Doves (pigeons), and Common Ground Doves are primarily ground feeders. They rarely open a shell, and so prefer seeds that they can swallow easily. White proso millet is the favorite of this family; black oil sunflower is also high on the list. Being fairly large, these common feeder birds prefer ground feeders, platform/fly-through feeders, and large hopper feeders.

BLUE JAY

JAYS: The quintessential feeder bandits (of the avian world, anyway) will come crashing in to feeders for peanuts. They seem to prefer the ones in the shell, picking up the whole peanuts one at a time, as if to check the weight to see if it's worth the effort of opening. They will also feed on peanut kernels, other nutmeats, sunflower seeds, and, occasionally, suet.

WOODPECKERS, FLICKERS, AND SAPSUCKERS: These tree-clinging birds can all be attracted to your yard with suet. It is important to initially offer suet on the trunk of a tree so that the birds find it more easily. Downy Woodpeckers can be attracted to sunflower chips, as can Northern Flickers. Hairy Woodpeckers, Red-bellied Woodpeckers, Downy Woodpeckers, and Red-headed Woodpeckers can also be enticed to peanut feeders. Because most of these birds are fairly large, a good-size hopper feeder or platform/fly-through style feeder best caters to them.

RED-BELLIED WOODPECKER

NUTHATCHES: As their name implies, nuthatches are fond of nuts and will be attracted to peanut feeders. They will also visit virtually any feeder loaded with black oil sunflower or sunflower chips. Due to their odd anatomical makeup (not being able to reach its own feet due to being a short, squat bird with very little neck), whatever a nuthatch grabs in its beak it must fly away with. It finds a crack or cranny in the bark of a nearby tree, jams the food into it, and hammers away to eat.

RED-BREASTED NUTHATCH

SPARROWS, JUNCOS, TOWHEES, AND BUNTINGS: Prefer ground feeders and large open platforms to most any other design. Their food of choice is white proso millet. Indigo Buntings have been known to occasionally visit a thistle feeder. Sunflower chips and peanut kernels can also be fed as an added attractant.

FOX SPARROW

HUMMINGBIRDS: Hummers are attracted to one type of feeder, one that dispenses sugar water. What is additionally important to note is that you can greatly increase your chances of attracting hummingbirds by planting and/or hanging plants native to your area that would attract hummingbirds. Plants that are most effective include Trumpet Vine, Honeysuckle, Impatiens, Fuchsia, Sweet William, Hibiscus, Butterfly Bush, Scarlet Sage, and Bee Balm. Check with your local nursery for the plantings best suited to your climate.

RUFOUS HUMMINGBIRD

FEEDING PREFERENCES OF SOME COMMON BIRDS*

Birds	Black Oil	Striped Sunflwr	White Millet	Nyjer	Hulled Snflwr	Peanut Kernels	Nectar	Suet
House Finch	5	3	2	3	5	1	0	0
Purple Finch	5	3	1	3	5	1	0	0
Carolina Chickadee	5	2	1	2	5	5	0	3
Black-capped Chickadee	5	5	2	1	2	5	0	3
Mountain Chickadee	5	2	1	2	5	5	0	3
Chestnut-backed Chickadee	5	5	3	1	5	5	0	3
Tufted Titmouse	5	3	0	0	4	5	0	4
Bushtit	5	2	1	0	4	4	0	3
Oak/Juniper Titmouse	5	3	0	0	4	4	0	3
American Goldfinch	4	2	1	4	5	0	0	0
Pine Siskin	3	0	0	5	4	0	0	0
Lesser Goldfinch	4	2	0	4	5	0	0	0
Common Redpoll	0	0	0	5	4	0	0	0
Northern Cardinal	5	4	1	0	5	4	0	0
Rose-breasted Grosbeak	5	5	0	0	4	2	0	0
Evening Grosbeak	5	5	0	0	3	1	0	0
Blue Grosbeak	5	5	0	0	3	1	0	0
Black-headed Grosbeak	5	5	0	0	3	1	0	0
Mourning Dove	3	2	5	3	3	1	0	0
Rock Dove (Pigeon)	4	2	5	2	3	2	0	0
Common Ground Dove	3	2	5	2	3	0	0	0
Blue Jay	4	3	2	0	3	5	0	2
Steller's Jay	3	3	2	0	2	5	0	2
Downy Woodpecker	3	2	0	0	4	5	0	5
Hairy Woodpecker	2	2	0	0	3	3	0	5
Red-bellied Woodpecker	3	3	0	0	4	5	0	5
Red-headed Woodpecker	2	2	0	0	3	5	0	5
Northern Flicker	2	2	0	0	4	4	0	5
Yellow-bellied Sapsucker	2	0	0	0	3	4	0	5
White-breasted Nuthatch	4	2	0	0	4	5	0	5
Red-breasted Nuthatch	4	0	0	0	3	5	0	4
Brown Creeper	0	0	0	0	2	1	0	5
Indigo Bunting	2	0	5	4	4	0	0	0
Painted Bunting	2	0	5	3	3	0	0	0
Eastern Towhee	3	2	5	0	3	4	0	0
American Tree Sparrow	3	2	5	2	4	2	0	0
Chipping Sparrow	2	0	5	2	3	0	0	0
White-throated Sparrow	2	2	5	1	3	5	0	0
Dark-eyed Junco	2	0	5	3	3	1	0	0
White-crowned Sparrow	2	0	5	0	3	3	0	0
Song Sparrow	2	1	5	3	4	3	0	0
Fox Sparrow	3	1	5	0	3	3	0	0
Common Grackle	4	5	3	0	3	4	0	3
European Starling	3	2	4	0	4	5	0	5
Brown-headed Cowbird	2	1	5	1	3	0	0	3
Red-winged Blackbird	3	2	5	0	3	2	0	0
Yellow-headed Blackbird	3	2	5	0	3	1	0	0
California Quail	2	1	5	1	3	1	0	0
Hummingbirds (most species)	0	0	0	0	0	0	5	0

* High Interest = 5, Low Interest = 0

Northern Cardinals are perhaps one of the most appreciated backyard birds—and very easy to attract to hopper or platform feeders.

Trumpet Creeper is attractive, easy to grow, and draws hummingbirds, but it may be invasive.

Chapter Five

THE BIG PICTURE

Although the addition of an efficient feeding station can greatly enhance your enjoyment of the birds in and around your yard, it is far from being the only way to attract birds. As mentioned earlier, the percentage of birds that visit your feeders represents only a fraction of the birdlife throughout the country.

Water

One need that all birds have no matter where you live is water. All birds must drink and bathe regularly, even in the coldest of temperatures. Adding a birdbath or some other water feature can attract an even greater number of species to your yard than just feeders—and you don't have to stop at just a birdbath.

In the desert, water draws more birds than does seed. This Bridled Titmouse is drinking from the faucet.

The variety of "bird-watering" products is larger today than it's ever been. From ponds that recirculate water through a waterfall rock to misters and drippers that connect to your outdoor water source and either drip or spray water in and around your birdbath and garden, your choices are virtually limitless. Let your imagination go wild and you will be rewarded with more birds than could ever visit your feeders. There are very few things in life as exuberant as an American Robin that finds a birdbath to its liking, as it dunks its head under the water, lets it roll down its back and shakes vigorously. The addition of water to your yard is vital to attracting birds like warblers, thrushes, vireos, orioles, and tanagers, as well as your regular visitors.

Brush Piles

Believe it or not, a heap of downed tree limbs, old Christmas trees, and the like can also enhance your habitat. Birds of the sparrow family especially find brush piles attractive places to both forage for food and build nests and rear young. Obviously, it is best that you put your brush pile somewhere unobtrusive so as not to offend the sensibilities of your neighbors, but there are few things you can add to your yard that will attract more birds per square foot than a big messy tangle of branches. Just pile them up and watch the birds weave their way in among the branches.

The backyard brush pile need not be unsightly.

Nesting Boxes

Nesting boxes are yet another addition to the "bird-friendly" backyard that can add some diversity and interest to your growing list of yard visitors. Nest boxes (although commonly referred to as "birdhouses," birds don't actually live in these boxes) are designed for birds that would normally nest in either naturally occurring tree cavities or those abandoned by woodpeckers from previous years. In our yards and suburbs, there are fewer and fewer places for these birds to raise their children. A well-constructed nest box can provide these birds with the essential elements for their nesting. Look for nest boxes that are not painted or stained. Raw wood is always best; remember, you are trying to replicate a tree cavity as closely as possible. As with wooden feeders, look for cedar construction, plenty of drainage in the bottom, and ventilation at the top. But, of all the ingredients that make up a

Regardless of style, some part of any nesting box must open for yearly cleaning.

good nesting box, the most crucial one is its ability to be cleaned out. Cleaning is usually accomplished by swinging out either the side or front so you can remove the old nest once the birds are finished with it. This way it is ready for another tenant and it will not become insect-infested over the summer.

Plantings

If you'd like to add even more for the birds in your yard, break out your shovel and garden tools and try some shrubs, vines, and trees. Plantings can provide food in the way of fruit and buds, cover from inclement weather and predators, and nectar for hummingbirds; they also add to the overall beauty of your yard. It is always best to check with as many resources as possible when undertaking a bird garden. Which birds are in your area and what plants will thrive there can make all the difference in the world.

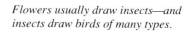

Flowers usually draw insects—and insects draw birds of many types.

Though cluttered, this yard should be excellent for attracting and holding many birds.

Chapter Six

THE CARE AND CLEANING OF YOUR FEEDING STATION

A lthough it may seem a bit basic, there is more to maintaining your feeding station than simply filling your feeders. Birdseed is messy, and birds are sloppy eaters. This situation requires attention on your part.

About once a season (four times a year) you should take your feeders down and wash them well. The preferred way to do this is with a strong white vinegar and hot water solution. Bleach, even in its most diluted state, is still toxic and really ought not to be used to clean feeders. Vinegar is nature's disinfectant and will leave no residue, nor will it discolor your feeders. Use a long-handled brush to get down into the insides of your tube feeders.

In fact, most birdfeeding specialty shops carry special bottlebrushes for just this purpose. Hopper feeders should have one side of the Plexiglas hopper removed, scrubbed out with a stiff brush, and allowed to dry overnight. The next morning, replace your feeders and fill them up.

Birdbaths should also be cleaned regularly with a hot water and vinegar solution. This should be done more frequently than with feeders, as baths tend to get a lot messier than feeders do.

You should also try and keep a handle on the piles of empty hulls beneath your feeders. Sunflower seed hulls are exceedingly acidic and don't let very much grow where they fall. Rake them up and dispose of them as you would any other yard waste; you can also use a shop vacuum to suck up the debris and then dispose of it the same way. Obviously, this is more for warm weather maintenance than winter.

Birdseed should always be stored in a way to discourage "undesirable" visitors. Mice, squirrels, raccoons, opossums, skunks, and about everything else that lives in your yard would be quite pleased to discover your cache of birdseed. It is best stored in a garage or shed in metal containers. A galvanized steel trash can makes the perfect seed container for your extra rations.

FALSE: BIRDS' FEET WILL FREEZE TO METAL PERCHES

Birds' feet are dry and scaly, more like bone than our skin. They are not inherently moist, so they will not freeze on contact with cold metal. Imagine how long you would have to leave a chicken bone on a piece of metal to get it to freeze there. The plastic perch covers sold in many stores are strictly a marketing item.

That cute little chipmunk can make off with more seeds than you might expect—and gnaw a hole in your feeder in the process.

A female Red-bellied Woodpecker, one of the most wide-ranging eastern U.S. woodpeckers, and perhaps the most common.

Feeding time for momma Carolina Chickadee.

Chapter Seven

READY TO FEED THE BIRDS

Your feeder is set up, you've filled it with a high quality birdseed, and you're sitting at your kitchen window thinking "Where are all the birds?" One thing to bear in mind is that birds do not automatically recognize a feeder as a food source. It can take a couple of weeks for them to warm up to a new feeder. One of the most important ingredients in any feeding station is patience. Give the birds a chance; they'll show up.

You may want to keep a pair of binoculars by your window, along with a field guide to birds of your area. A good pair of binoculars can go a long way to enhancing your experience with the birds in your

Birdfeeding Myths

You shouldn't feed birds during the warmer weather

There is no sound scientific data to support this theory. In fact, it is during the warmer weather that birds are establishing territories, attracting mates, building and defending nests. The breeding season is a time of great stress for birds; during this period our feeders become the avian equivalent of a fast food restaurant, a quick bite to eat for overworked parents. Also, if you suspend birdfeeding outside of the winter, you miss the migratory visitors as they pass through your area as well as the young birds that could be taught that your yard is a good place to visit. In many parts of the country, spring and summer are also the seasons that offer the only opportunity to see hummingbirds. So, if you enjoy feeding your birds, feel free to do so all year long.

Birds won't migrate when they are supposed to if there is food available

We actually know very little about what triggers bird migration. It is apparent, however, that it is not tied to food supplies. Many migratory birds begin their migration while there are still ample food supplies on their breeding grounds. A few pounds of sunflower seeds are not going to derail thousands of years of evolution. In addition, a high percentage of the birds that use birdfeeders are year-round residents of your area.

Hummingbird nectar must be red to be effective

This is one myth that just won't go away. If you could milk a flower that a hummingbird was visiting, you would find the nectar quite clear. A mixture of four or five parts water to one part ordinary table sugar, boiled well and cooled, is the appropriate recipe. No honey, no artificial sweeteners, and no dyes are to be used. Besides, any hummingbird feeder worth using will itself be more than red enough to attract the birds.

Suet should only be fed in winter

Back in the "old days" of birdfeeding, when suet was a slab of stringy fat you got from your local butcher, feeding suet in winter was a pretty good idea because the cold weather prevented the suet from going rancid. But, in this day of commercially prepared suets, the odds of it going bad are virtually nil. There are also "summer suets" or "suet doughs" that won't melt at all, no matter how hot it gets. Birds do eat suet in the warm weather; woodpeckers, chickadees, titmice, nuthatches, and even Gray Catbirds and Northern Mockingbirds will enjoy suet all year.

Once you start feeding birds, you cannot stop

Although during times of high stress, courtship, breeding, and a hard winter birdfeeding is helpful, the birds are not going to starve to death if you need to stop for whatever reason. The birds get only a small portion of their daily caloric and nutritional intake from birdseed. If you stop, the birds will continue as they had before you started. Birds are survivors; they have adapted to our environment but have not become overly dependent on humans.

The more variety of seed I put out, the more variety of birds I will attract

Nope. No matter how exotic the mixture may appear, birds won't eat just anything that is offered. Keep your seed offerings simple: black oil sunflower, black stripe sunflower, peanuts, and white proso millet. That's about it. The addition of dried pressed fruit nuggets and the like will not bring birds that are not "feeder birds" into your station.

backyard. You should find a pair that are either seven or eight power with an objective lens size (the second number in every binoculars specification) of 30 millimeters or more. It's best if they have a field of view of at least 350 feet at 1,000 yards and a close focusing distance of at least 15 feet. The binoculars should be lightweight and easy to hold and focus. Stay away from gimmick-type options on binoculars, such as zooms, "zip," or "perma focus." Most importantly, buy binoculars that fit. If they are uncomfortable or too heavy or you are unable to focus on one image when you look through them, try another pair.

Another useful birding tool is a field guide to the birds of your area. Most field guides in this country are divided into eastern and western regions. The most important thing about a field guide is to read it. Become familiar with where certain types of birds are listed and read the descriptions of them. This is a terrific way to learn more about the birds in and around your yard.

Now you are ready to feed the birds. Welcome to a world of color, song, and fascination. Although this guide covers many topics, it is by no means totally complete. The one thing that can be said about Mother Nature is that there are no absolutes. The most important thing is to remember to enjoy yourself. Birdfeeding is a hobby that can last a lifetime and be passed down from generation to generation.

Good Birding!

Some birds, like these Red Crossbills, are difficult to find except at feeders during the winter. A good feeder can give you color, rarity, and simple enjoyment of birds.

RESOURCES

Organizations

NATIONAL AUDUBON SOCIETY
700 Broadway
New York, NY 10003
212-979-3000

CORNELL LAB OF ORNITHOLOGY
Membership Department
P.O. Box 11
Ithaca, NY 14851
607-254-2425
www.ornith.cornell.edu/

NEW JERSEY AUDUBON SOCIETY
9 Hardscrabble Rd.
Bernardsville, NJ 07924

CAPE MAY BIRD OBSERVATORY-CENTER FOR RES. & EDUC.
600 Route 47 N.
Cape May Courthouse, NJ 08210
609-861-0700

CAPE MAY BIRD OBSERVATORY-NORTHWOOD CENTER
P.O. Box 3
701 E. Lake Dr.
Cape May Point, NJ 08212
609-861-0466

AMERICAN BIRDING ASSOCIATION
P.O. Box 6599
Colorado Springs, CO 80934
719-578-1614
www.americanbirding.org

SOUTHEASTERN ARIZONA BIRD OBSERVATORY
P.O. Box 5521
Bisbee, AZ 85603

Magazines and Periodicals

BIRDER'S WORLD
P.O. Box 1612
Waukesha, WI 53187-1612
1-800-446-5489

BIRD WATCHER'S DIGEST
P.O. Box 110
Marietta, OH 45750
1-800-879-2473

WILDBIRD
Subscription Department
P.O. Box 52898
Boulder, CO 80323-2898

Feeder Manufacturers & Retailers

DROLL YANKEES
27 Mill Road
Foster, RI 02825

ARUNDALE PRODUCTS
Mandarin Feeders

BACKYARD NATURE PRODUCTS
Bird Stuff/Wood Country
Chilton, WI

C&S PRODUCTS

HEATH FEEDERS AND FEED

WILD BIRD CENTERS OF AMERICA
7370 MacArthur Blvd.
Glen Echo, MD 20812
1-800-WILD-BIRD

Optics for Birding

BUSHNELL SPORT OPTICS
9200 Cody
Overland Park, KS 66214
1-800-423-3537

KOWA OPTIMED
2001 S. Vermont Ave.
Torrance, CA 90502
1-800-966-5692

LEICA CAMERA
156 Ludlow Ave.
Northvale, NJ 07647

NIKON
1300 Walt Whitman Road
Melville, NY 11747
516-547-4200
1-800-NIKON-US

SWAROVSKI OPTIK
2 Slater Dr.
Cranston, RI 02920
1-800-426-3089

SWIFT INSTRUMENTS
952 Dorchester Ave.
Boston, MA 02125
1-800-446-1116

ZEISS OPTICALS
1015 Commerce St.
Petersburg, VA 23803
1-800-338-2984

INDEX

Page numbers in **bold** indicate photos